This journal belongs to:

New Moon

Fresh Starts, New Plans,
Brainstorming

AQUARIUS

Waxing Crescent

Set Intentions- Write out
hopes, wishes and dreams

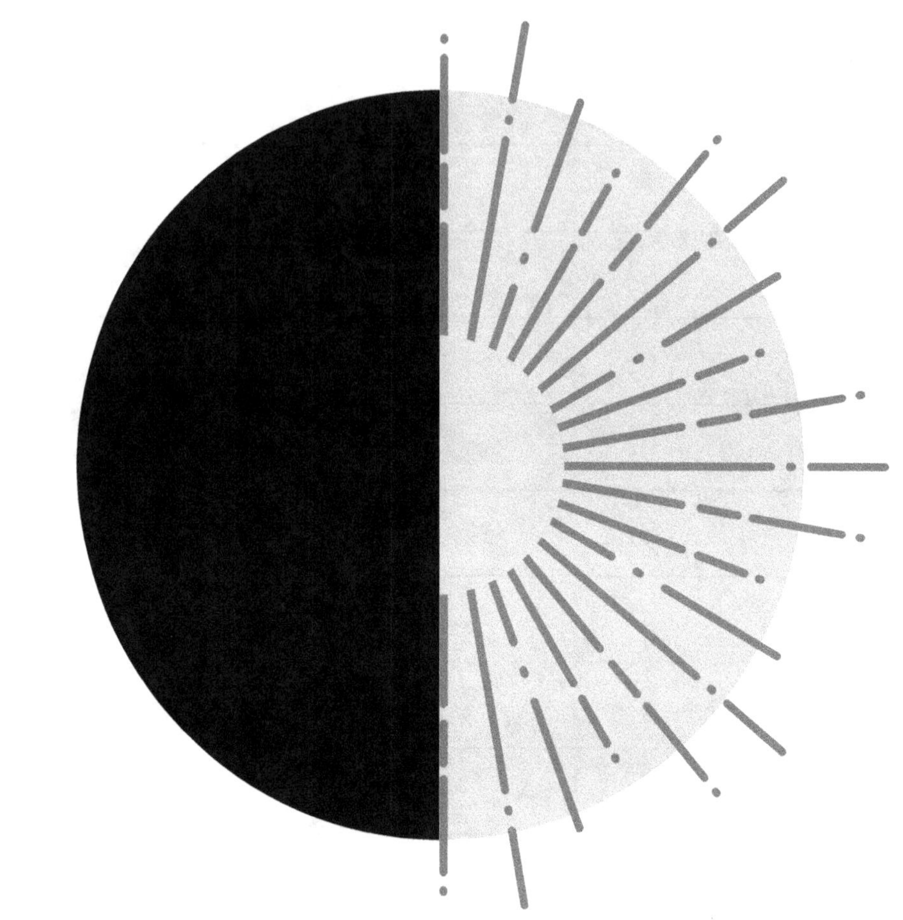

First Quarter Moon

Pedal to the Metal,
Boots on the Ground
Take Action

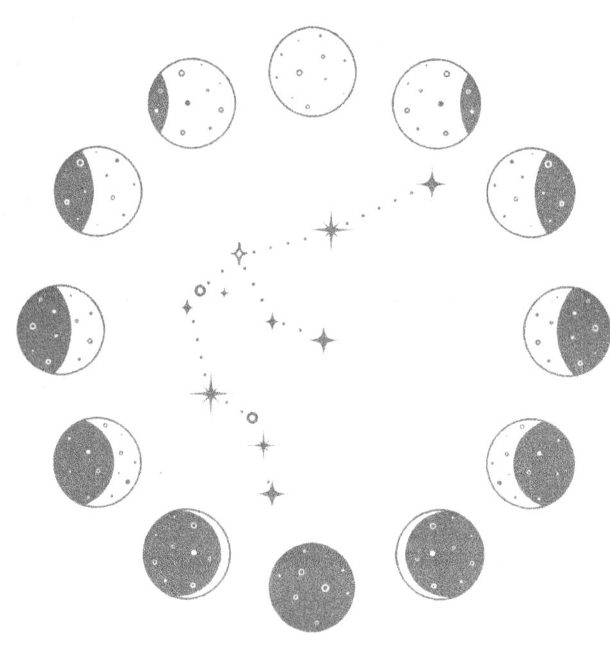

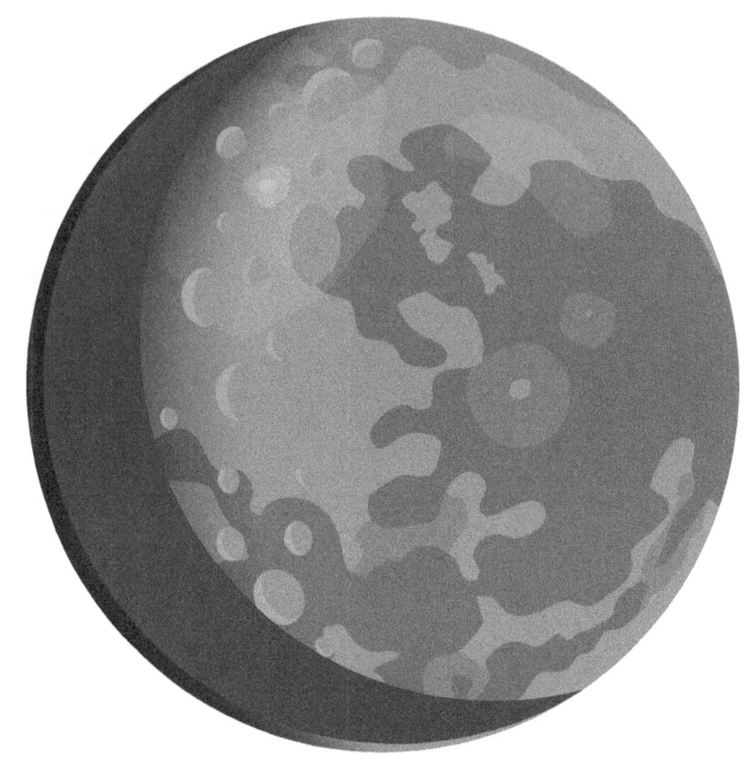

Waxing Gibbous Moon

Look for snippets of the manifestation and focus on those to grow them

Full Moon

Enjoy the harvest of your intentions from the previous moon cycle

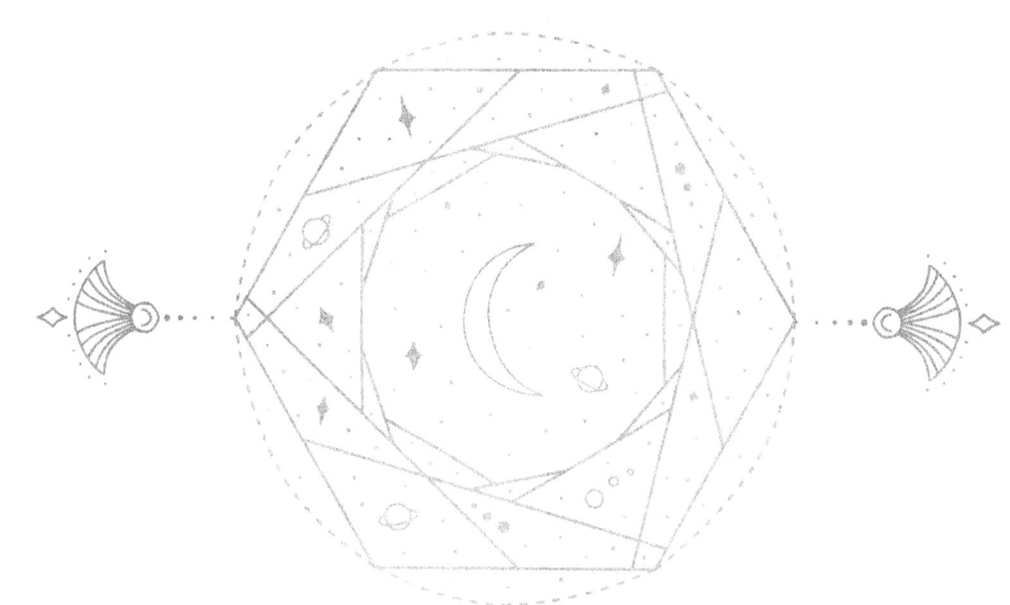

Waning Gibbous Moon

Gratefulness rules - Self care
and reflection time

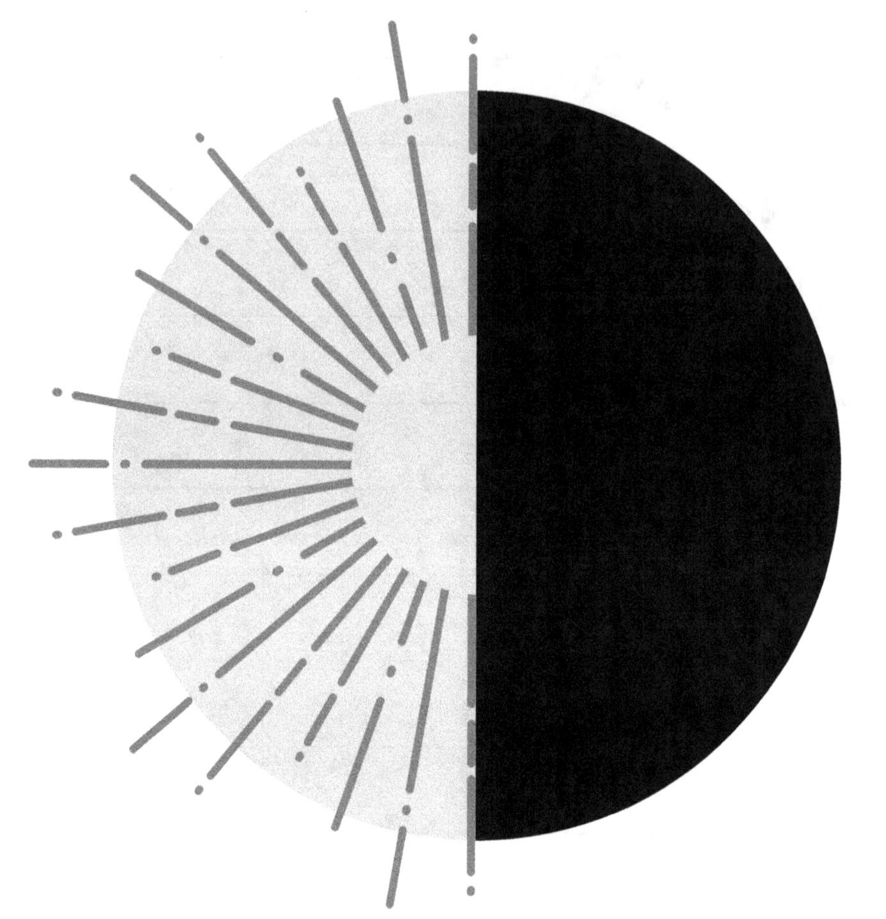

Third Quarter Moon

Make space for new
arrivals that serve you

Waning Crescent

Rest; and let it flow in

Aquarius

New Moon

New Beginnings
Sage your self and space

Things to remember:

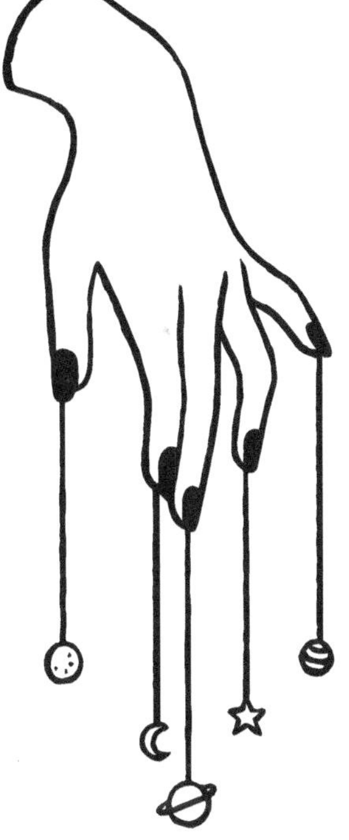